THURGOOD

George Stevens, Jr

BROADWAY PLAY PUBLISHING INC
224 E 62nd St, NY, NY 10065
www.broadwayplaypub.com
info@broadwayplaypub.com

First printing: April 2014
Second printing: March 2015
I S B N: 978-0-88145-592-2

Book design: Marie Donovan
Page make-up: Adobe Indesign
Typeface: Palatino
Printed and bound in the U S A

THURGOOD was first performed at the Westport Country Playhouse on 11 May 2006, starring James Earl Jones.

THURGOOD premiered on Broadway at the Booth Theater on 30 April 2008. It was produced by Vernon Jordan, The Shubert Organization, Bill Rollnick/ Nancy Ellison Rollnick, Matt Murphy, Daryl Roth/ Debra Black, Roy Furman, Jam Theatricals, Lawrence Horowitz, Eric Falkenstein, Max Onstage, James D'Orta, Jamie deRoy, Amy Nederlander in association with Ostar Productions and The Westport Country Playhouse. The cast and creative contributors were:

THURGOOD	Laurence Fishburne
Director	Leonard Foglia
Scenic Design	Allen Moyer
Costume Design	Jane Greenwood
Lighting Design	Brian Nason
Projection Design	Elaine McCarthy
Sound Design	Ryan Rummery
Production Stage Manager	Marti McIntosh

Subsequent productions:

June 3, 2010—Eisenhower Theater, The Kennedy Center, Washington, DC. Cast: Laurence Fishburne

July 7, 2010—Geffen Playhouse, Los Angeles, CA. Cast: Laurence Fishburne

March 7, 2013—Pittsburgh Public Theater, Pittsburgh, PA. Cast: Montae Russell

December 11, 2013—Florida Studio Theatre, Sarasota, FL. Cast: Montae Russell

PREFACE

Thurgood Marshall was one of the defining American characters of the 20th Century. His story is heroic because he changed history, deploying the law like an army, challenging his country to live up to the principles upon which it was founded. He was the architect of successful court challenges to existing law that became the foundation for the civil rights movement. Marshall offers the playwright the gift of his own humanity and humor. His Supreme Court colleague Justice William Brennan observed that Marshall's anecdotes, often dealing with the grimmer moments of his life, were his way of purging the bleakest times while preserving the history.

Bill Haber read my play and told me he wanted to produce it on Broadway. Bill had a strong belief in the themes of the play and he was steadfast in seeing that it was produced with integrity.

(A long table with upright leather armchairs and a small lectern. The back wall may be used for projections of photos and images. A sign over the proscenium: Howard University Law School)

(A tall man, aided by a cane, enters wearing a slightly rumpled blue suit that suggests he is not preoccupied by appearance. He surveys the scene through horn-rimmed glasses...remembering. He speaks with the assurance of a man accustomed to advancing a point of view.)

THURGOOD MARSHALL: Well, we might as well get right down to it. I've given fifty years to the law. I've seen a lot and I've gotten too old to keep secrets. Here at Howard University, we were taught one simple idea—the law is a weapon if you know how to use it. I was here during the Great Depression—class of 1933. You've got this fancy auditorium now—even a chandelier. We had an old three-story brownstone with no heat—and nobody knew what air-conditioning was back then. I'd take the train over from Baltimore every morning, arrive at Union Station and some days I'd walk past the United States Capitol on my way to class.

People call Baltimore "up south" —just below what we used to call the Smith and Wesson line. Baltimore was where slaves ran to when they escaped from plantations in the Deep South—which may have something to do with why I was born there.

My Uncle Fearless used to tell me about my great grandfather who was called Thorney Good. Seems, as a boy, he was a tracker for a big-game hunter in the toughest part of the Congo and this big-game hunter brought my great-grandfather to eastern Maryland—as a slave. Now Thorney Good hated being a slave. He became so hard to handle the big game hunter got fed up and said:

"Look, I brought you over here myself so I don't guess I can shoot you like you deserve—but you're so ornery to white people I can't sell you. I can't even give you away. So I'm going to set you free, provided you get the hell off this Eastern Shore and never come back."

And that was the only time the big game hunter didn't get an argument from Thorny Good.

But years later he did come back and bought land right next door so he could torment the big-game hunter for the rest of his life.

My grandfather's name was Thoroughgood Marshall. He had a grocery store on the corner of Dolphin and Division, and Grandma Annie Marshall was the lady of the store. One day the electric company decides to put a power pole right in front of the store. When the workmen come with a court order, Annie Marshall takes an old cane backed kitchen chair out on the sidewalk, plunks herself down right on the spot. She sits there for four days and four nights until she gets her way. They say Grandma Annie's was the first successful sit-down strike in the history of Maryland.

My mother's father was named Isaiah Olive Branch Williams. He came back from the Merchant Marines and started a family—a boy and a girl—Avon and Avonia, named after Shakespeare's river; Denmedia Marketa—for the family store; my mother Norma—for Bellini's opera; My Uncle Fearless—for the way he glared at his daddy right after he was born.

As a boy I came to understand that two things marked my family—distinctive names and extreme stubbornness.

My parents named me after my grandfather, Thoroughgood. *(Spells it.)* T H O R O U G H G O O D. By second grade I got tired of writing out all those letters—so I cut it to Thurgood.

I was born in 1908—the year that William Howard Taft was elected President and the year Jack Johnson knocked out Tommy Burns. A Negro was heavyweight champion of the world. But you know what happened the very next day? They started looking for 'the great white hope' to take back the title.

There were race riots in Springfield, Illinois—the home of Abraham Lincoln. Eighty-nine Negroes were lynched that year. That's when they started the N A A C P —the National Association for the Advancement of Colored People.

(THURGOOD studies the audience.)

How many of you've heard of Homer Adolph Plessy?

After the Civil War Homer Plessy and other Negroes in the South had been free to vote and sit anywhere they damn well pleased—and then in 1890 Louisiana passed a law that ordered rail companies to provide separate accommodations for white people and colored people. You know what they called it? *(He plays the irony.)* "An Act to Promote the Comfort of Passengers." Homer Plessy decides to challenge this law by taking a seat in a whites-only coach outside New Orleans. He refuses to move to the colored car so they arrest him, haul him in to Criminal District Court. Homer Plessy says the segregation law is a violation of his rights under the Fourteenth Amendment to the Constitution. Judge John H Ferguson doesn't see it that way. He fines him twenty-five dollars.

Well, Homer Plessy refused to pay the twenty-five dollars and he and his lawyer took it all the way to the Supreme Court of the United States.

The case was called Plessy v. Ferguson.

The Supreme Court ruled seven to one against Mister Plessy.

(He goes upstage to the table and removes a document from a weathered leather briefcase.)

Listen to what the justices wrote: "The Fourteenth Amendment could not have been intended to enforce social equality. The feelings of inferiority that come from being segregated exist only because the colored race chooses to put that construction on it."

What did that mean? It meant it was now legal for any state to pass Jim Crow laws that forced Negroes to accept "separate but equal" facilities.

When I was growing up in Baltimore we had to use separate drinking fountains, separate park benches and separate public toilets.

If you want to understand my story, don't forget that name—Homer Adolph Plessy.

(A train whistle sounds in the distance. THURGOOD *turns, walks upstage, places his cane on the table and removes his glasses. A projection of Pullman waiters in white starched jackets fills the back wall. He goes deeper into his memory and we sense a youthful vitality.)*

My Daddy was a Pullman car waiter on the B & O Railroad. He had blond hair and blue eyes and sometimes people mistook him for a white man.
He was the most insidious of my family of rebels.
He taught me how to argue and debate—he challenged my logic on every point, even when we were discussing the weather.

He didn't have much schooling, he was angry and he was a drinker—but somehow he became interested in the law. His hobby was to go downtown and sit in the back of the courthouse, and some days he'd carry me with him. When we came home, he'd knock back a few shots of whisky and test me on the cases at the dinner table. We would have the most violent arguments you ever heard.

He had his own way of making his points. He'd say things like,

"Ahh, that's mighty black of you."

Or, "There must be a white man in the woodpile."

One day he sat me down... "Thurgood, if anybody calls you a nigger, you have business with them right then and there. Either win or lose right then and there."

(A trolley sound, he gets to his feet. Image of a crowded streetcar in downtown Baltimore.)

I got an after school job working for Mister Schoen, a Jewish gentleman who ran a fancy dress shop on Charles Street. One afternoon he sends me to deliver a big pile of hats during the rush hour. I go to get on the trolley when a woman pushes past me. Then I feel a hand grab my collar and this white man pulls me off the trolley. "Sir, I'm just trying to get on the damned car."

He says, "Nigger, don't you push in front of white people!"

Well, I started swinging. The man smacks me to the ground and tramples all over the hats. A policeman hauls me down to the station. I call Mister Schoen and he comes over to the jail. I'm crying by that time and I apologize for the damage to the hats.

He says, "That man really call you a nigger?"

Yes, sir, he sure did.

"Thurgood, you forget about the damn hats, you did the right thing."

You ever hear of Colored High? That's where I went. The same school my mother went to. I had the habit of saying whatever was on my mind and I'd end up in arguments. One day my teacher says in front of the whole class, "Thurgood, you are *disputatious!*" Then she hands me a copy of the Constitution of the United States and sends me down to the furnace room to memorize some part of it. This was her special punishment for me. I was sent to the furnace room so often, by my senior year I knew the whole thing by heart.

(THURGOOD *moves to stage left and looks out the window. Sounds of police and prisoners)*

From our second story classroom window, I could look right down on the Northwest Baltimore Police Station. I'd watch Negro prisoners brought in by the white policemen.

(Remembering…violent!)

"Black boy, why don't you just shut your goddamned mouth!"

"Nigger, you're going to talk yourself into the electric chair!"

To this day, I can't get it out of my head—the sound of those cops beating the hell out of those Negro prisoners.

My mother was set on me getting a college education, so I had to earn some money. Uncle Fearless got me a job—as a dining car waiter on the B & O.

They gave me this uniform—the pants were about six inches too short. I go to the steward and ask him if

I can get a longer pair of pants. He says, "Don't you know it's easier for me to find a shorter nigger than it is for me to get a longer pair of pants? Why don't you just scroonch down in them."

So I scroonched down in them and became a pretty good waiter. I bet I'm the only one here who can bone and serve a trout on a moving train without putting any in the customer's lap.

(A projection of alluring 1930s co-eds in stylish hats covers the back wall.)

I arrived at Lincoln College with a comic book in my back pocket and a highly cultivated interest in the female gender.

I was pinned to seven co-eds. All at the same time! I'd already decided to become a dentist and never lift anything heavier than a poker chip.

Then one day we go in to town to see a movie and after we buy our tickets, they tell us we have to go around to the back and up the stairs to sit in the colored balcony—the crow's nest.

I'll tell you something. If enforcement hadn't been so such a problem they would have made a law that said, "white folks get to laugh first".

We asked for our quarters back and they refused. We got angry and pulled down a bunch of curtains and broke a door and ran like hell.

We were kind of pleased with ourselves, but that night I couldn't sleep. I lay there thinking, am I going to go through life being humiliated because of the color of my skin?

One of the boys was named Langston Hughes. Yes, Langston Hughes—he was already writing poetry.

You see, Lincoln was an all-Negro college with all white professors, and Langston was a fighter. He'd organized a campaign to get Lincoln to hire some Negro professors. The next day I went to Langston and said, "I want to work with you."

We had our first Negro professor within a year and I learned something from Langston—one person *can* make a difference. He got me committed. I put away the comic books, stopped playing pinochle, started reading history and joined the debate team.

And then one day I met the most beautiful and smart and sensitive seventeen year old co-ed you ever saw. Everyone called her Buster. I told Buster she could wear my pin. Buster informed me that I was going to marry her.

And that's just what I did.

By then I knew I wanted to go to law school, so I got out my white jacket to go make some money at the Gibson Island Club, where my daddy was the head waiter.

(Period music. A projection of an elegant Southern dining club.)

One night a United States Senator—a very crude individual—comes in with a bevy of beautiful women and sits down at a table under a portrait of some great confederate general. He spots me.

He says, "Hey, nigger." Now I don't like the idea of his calling me that, not one bit. But I go over. "Nigger, I want service at this table." Well, I give him the service and he keeps callin' me that and I'm liking it less and less. But when he gets up he lays twenty dollars on the table. Now this crude fellah keeps comin' to the club and keeps on leaving me twenty-dollar tips. Those twenties added up.

One night my daddy hears this senator saying, "Hey nigger…" nigger this and nigger that, and sees me running over and taking good care of him. My daddy's blue eyes were on fire.

"Thurgood, you're fired! You're a disgrace to colored people."

Well, after Daddy cooled down I explained what was goin' on.

(He moves downstage, closer to the audience.)

Now, between you and me, anytime, you want to call me nigger, you just lay your twenty dollars on the table. And you can keep on doin' it all day long.

But, the second you run out of them twenties, I'm gonna have business with you right then and there.

The University of Maryland Law School was just a ten-minute trolley ride from our house. But even though we paid taxes in Maryland, they wouldn't accept my application. And the Plessy decision meant they didn't have to. I told Mama, "Some day I'm gonna get even".

The only other choice was here at Howard University. You know what they called Howard in those days? "The dummy's retreat."

I hadn't earned enough waiting tables, so—and I didn't know this 'til years later—my mother took the bus downtown and pawned her engagement ring and wedding band so I could study here.

Charles Hamilton Houston took over the Law School the year I got here. Charlie Houston was smart as a whip and handsome as a movie star. He'd been an officer in the Army in World War One and was the first Negro editor of the Harvard Law Review.

Charlie Houston stormed into class that first day,
wearing his Phi Beta Kappa key—slammed the door
behind him!

"Look at the man on your right. Now look at the man
on your left—and understand this: Two of you won't
be here next year. I am here to make Howard into the
West Point of Negro leadership. Think about this, there
are one hundred and sixty thousand white lawyers
in America and less than a thousand Negro lawyers
and we are going to change that. I want you to learn
what your rights are under the Constitution, regardless
of how they've been interpreted by the courts, and
to use the law to obtain justice. When you go into a
courtroom, you cannot say— "Please, Mister Court,
have mercy upon me because I am a Negro". You will
be in competition with a highly trained white lawyer
and if you expect to win, you'd better be better than he
is. If I give you five cases to read overnight, you better
read eight. And when I say eight, you better read ten.
You go that step further and you just might make it."

No one ever challenged me before. Now, a great
human being was saying, "Shape up or ship out". I
was *not* going to ship out.

Some days I'd take the trolley across town to the
Supreme Court building, walk up those steps and look
at the words carved in stone, "Equal Justice Under
Law". I'd go inside, stand in the back of that chamber
and listen to the great lawyers…like John W Davis,
the one they called the lawyer's lawyer. He would
talk in those smooth Southern cadences and get all
nine justices in the palm of his hand. I could feel in my
bones the power and the majesty of the law.

The summer of 1933, Charlie Houston asked me to
drive down south with him in his beat-up jalopy
to study school conditions, me sitting in the back

seat taking notes with a typewriter on my lap. It's a hundred degrees and we're not allowed in restaurants so we'd pack our lunch. One day I sit under a tree and a little boy comes over and he's hungry.

So I offer him half my sandwich, but he keeps staring at this beautiful orange, which on this hot afternoon I'm really looking forward to.

Well, I hand him this beautiful orange. Next thing I know he's biting through the rind, smashing it in his face.

"Stop that! What do you think you're doing? Stop that!"

Now the little boy is frightened and starts to cry. Charlie comes running—thinking we've been attacked by the Klan.

"I'm sorry, Charlie. It's just that I'd been looking forward to that orange all day long."

"Look around you, Thurgood. Do you see that sharecropper shack? Do you see that doghouse school—dirt floors, no windows? This little boy has never seen an orange before. You're embarrassing yourself, and you're embarrassing me."

That night I wrote to my parents: "Dear Mom and Dad: I still have so much to learn. Professor Houston says a lawyer who is not a social engineer is a social parasite. I believe that is God's truth."

Charlie started talking about how to take on segregated schools. There were two ways. One way was to go into the courts and challenge it head on, arguing that segregation is unconstitutional. The other was to *use* the Plessy decision—separate but equal—to insist that the states provide truly equal schools for Negro students. We call that Jim Crow Deluxe.

So how do you start? Charlie decided we should start with university graduate schools. Find somebody who ain't afraid to stick his neck out and won't be intimidated. I found a fellow named Donald Gaines Murray who was an honor graduate from Amherst and he agreed to apply to the University of Maryland Law School.

I had a score to settle with those bastards.

(THURGOOD *goes to his briefcase and removes a letter.*)

"Dear Mr Murray...President Pearson instructed me to return your application and your two dollar money order. The University of Maryland does not accept Negro students. We maintain the Princess Anne Academy as a separate institution for the education of Negroes."

This was "Exhibit A".

We sue the University charging that by refusing Mister Murray's application they had violated the Fourteenth Amendment.

One Monday morning Charlie Houston, Donald Gaines Murray and I show up in Baltimore City Court in double-breasted suits with handkerchiefs in our breast pockets.

President Pearson started out by informing the court that there is an exceptional facility for the study of law available to Mister Murray down the road at Howard University. Well, the Dean of the Howard Law and his prize pupil were fixin' to show his ass just how right he was.

President Pearson, it is true, is it not, the University of Maryland does not admit Negroes?

You say the Princess Anne Academy offers the same caliber of education and the faculty is comparable.

Isn't it true Princess Anne has only one faculty member with a master's degree?

And the Dean uses the title "doctor", but the title is "honorary?"

Isn't it true the University of Maryland has prominent Baltimore judges teaching the laws of Maryland?

Then, if Mister Murray wishes to practice law in Maryland, how can any law school be equal to the University of Maryland?

Would you admit Mexicans, Japanese and Filipinos to your University?

You would? Then why, President Pearson, are members of Mister Murray's race not admitted?

I see..."because state policy decrees it".

No further questions.

(He turns to the court, making his closing argument.)

Your honor, the state of Maryland cites Plessy v. Ferguson and the doctrine of separate but equal to justify its segregation policy. But in this case we haven't challenged their right to have separate schools. Rather, we have proven that Maryland's separate school system is not equal. The Plessy decision is the law of the land—the law requires that Mister Murray be given an equal education.

At five o'clock on June 25th, 1935, we got called back into the courtroom. Judge Eugene O'Dunne hammers his gavel. He then orders the University of Maryland to admit Donald Gaines Murray to its law school.

Like Charlie Houston said, the law is a weapon. Okay, this may have been only one tiny crack in the great wall that stood between Negroes and the promised land, but that didn't keep Charlie Houston and me

from booting up a few. We closed quite a few saloons
that night.

Oh, I forgot to tell you—my mother was a Maryland
schoolteacher—a very fine schoolteacher. I would get
so goddamned mad that my mother—unlike white
teachers—was required to scrub the floors of her
classroom every night. And do you know what she
was paid? She was paid forty percent less than white
teachers. So we decided to take it to court.

This was my first case on my own so I was a little
nervous that day—they didn't see Negro lawyers much
in those courts. Now, when I invoked the Fourteenth
Amendment this hard assed judge stares down at me
and says, "Lawyer, do you have a copy with you?"
"No your honor, but I can tell you what it says."

(THURGOOD *recites:*)

"All persons born or naturalized in the United States
and subject to the jurisdiction thereof, are citizens of
the United States and of the State wherein they reside.
No State shall make or enforce any law which shall
abridge the privileges or immunities of citizens of the
United States; nor shall any State deprive any person
of life, liberty, or property, without due process of law;
nor deny to any person the equal protection of the
laws."

Do you know what the judge said, so help me God?
"Lawyer...as long as I've been on the bench, I didn't
know the Fourteenth Amendment applied to Negroes."

A few trips to the furnace room might have made that
man a better judge.

The court ruled that the difference in salary was
discrimination on account of race. The state of
Maryland knew it would cost them a bundle to fight
this out in every county, so they passed a law that

gave equal salaries to Negro teachers—including my mother, Mrs Norma Marshall.

(Jazz music—we see the New York City skyline.)

New York City. Charlie Houston offered me two hundred dollars a month to come work with him at the legal department of the N A A C P and I grabbed it. So Buster and I move to New York and we get ourselves a little apartment in Harlem. Our offices weren't fancy. You had to walk around the winos to get through the front door.

But, Charlie Huston had a *plan*. He said real political power in the South would never come until Negroes had a vote—a vote that meant something.

And, I'm thinking there are a million Negroes in Texas. If we get a million Negroes with votes that count, we're going to have some fun.

So, Charlie sent me down south. What I found there were all sorts of schemes that had just one purpose—to keep Negroes from voting. Poll taxes; "literacy" tests; physical intimidation. I got to Louisiana the day after a sheriff had shot and killed a Negro just for registering to vote. In Texas, Negroes could vote in the general election, but that meant nothing because Texas was a Democratic state so whoever wins the Democratic primary automatically gets elected—and Negroes weren't allowed to vote in the primary. That really fired me up!

So we went into the Texas courts—and do you know what the Democratic Party officials say?

They say their party is a private club and they were free to select the club's membership. And the Texas courts agreed with them.

But, one year later the Supreme Court of the United States agreed to hear our appeal. The case was called Smith v. Allwright.

I called Buster the morning the decision came down—April 3, 1944. Eight to one, honey, for us! Buster burst into tears.

Listen to what the justices wrote. "It is unconstitutional for a political party to limit its voters to white people because it endorses and enforces discrimination against Negroes."

You know what happened next?

The Negroes got dressed up in their Sunday best just to register to vote. It was a hundred degrees and they were standing in a long line and this white couple starts pushing to get ahead. This Negro woman holding a parasol turns to them:

"You seem to be in a hurry, so you just go right ahead. We've been waiting a long time—we don't mind waiting a little bit longer."

I knew our victory in the voting case was the beginning of real progress—without the ballot a man isn't a citizen. But I knew something else. The ballot doesn't mean much without a first class education.

Now, they used to say the reason white people didn't want to open the schoolhouse door is it will lead straight to the bedroom door. Well now, do I need to tell you that other door has been open a mighty long time?

In Baltimore I used to see kids play ball in the streets together, then separate to go to school. I'd see them come out of school and play ball together. It made me wonder, why do they have to be separated in school? I came to believe that children sitting in classrooms learning alongside one another was the best hope for our country. That's when I decided to go to Clarendon County, South Carolina.

You know the cold truth? Every time I got on a train down south I wasn't sure if I was coming back. There was no welcome mat for Negro lawyers. I'd take the Capitol Limited from New York to Washington DC, then I'd change to a 'colored' car for the rest of the trip.

In southern cities I'd sit in the back of streetcars—quiet as a mouse; and I'd eat in colored cafes.

They had me sleeping in a different house every night. I never wanted anyone to know that sometimes I'd lay on the bed sweating—wondering if I'd ever see Buster again. I'd picture my dead body laid out some place where they let white kids out of Sunday school to come look at me and rejoice.

I'll tell you a story. One time we're defending two Negroes charged with murder in a race riot in Columbia, Tennessee, near the birthplace of the Ku Klux Klan.

Word was out they'd kill us if we tried to sleep in that town, so we drive forty-five miles to Nashville every night. We're leaving town just after sunset. I spot three or four state police cars—and we're pulled over. I'm at the wheel.

(*Bright flashlights are shined in his face blinding him.*)

They say they have a warrant to search our car.

The Sheriff says, "Okay boys, check out the trunk".

I say to my people, "Don't let 'em plant something on us". Well, it was a dry county and they knew that lawyers are gonna drink. Now believe it or not we didn't have any whiskey in the car.

The sheriff says, "Search this nigger lawyer".

I say, "You got a warrant to search me?"

"No."

"Well, the answer is no."

He says, "*This* must be the one. You get out the car".

"What for?"

"Drunken driving."

"I haven't had a drink in twenty-four hours."

They shove me in a police car between two beefy deputies holding shotguns and drive off. Suddenly the car turns off the road and heads through the woods toward the river. We get to a place where a bunch of men are waiting under a big tree with a rope hanging over it—fixin' to do a little bit of lynching. Then the car with my friends shows up—so I guess these deputies get cold feet. They turn around and drive me to town.

The streets are empty. Hell, everybody's down by the river.

The sheriff says, "Alright nigger, the magistrate's in that building over yonder—you go ahead on."

I say, "You're not gonna shoot me in the back while I'm *escaping*, are you?"

He says, "Oh, smart ass nigger". And he takes me over.

The little magistrate is five foot nothing. He says, "What's up?"

"We got this boy for drunken driving."

"I'm not drunk."

"Do you want to take my test?"

"What's your test?"

"I'm a teetotaler—never had a drink in my life. I can smell liquor a mile off. Wanna' take a chance? Blow your breath on me."

I blew my breath so hard I rocked him!

"Hell, what are you boys talking about? This man hasn't had a drink…in twenty-four hours. Get out of here!"

I got myself on the fastest goddamn train out of there. And I had a *drink*. I sat with a bottle of Wild Turkey and thanked the lord. And I thought about the Negroes who stayed behind because they were the heroes. I met this preacher down there who told me he was not about to turn the other cheek. In the glove compartment of his car he had two items—a Bible and a .45. He told me, "I'll try the Bible first".

Anyway, I told you I was headed to Clarendon County, South Carolina.

The superintendent of schools had refused to provide a bus for the Scotts Branch School—a little one-room schoolhouse. We called 'em doghouse schools. Harry Briggs was a garage mechanic who fought in World War Two. His seven-year-old boy had to walk five miles to school every day. Briggs signed a complaint charging the school district with violating his son's rights to an equal education. The very next day the garage owner fired Briggs, and we took on the case.

Now, our case simply asked for equal school facilities, but Judge Waties Waring—a rare Southern maverick surprised us. He challenged us to address the larger question. Were South Carolina's segregated schools legal under the Constitution?

Judge Waring had forced our hand. So, now, instead of taking on one local school board, we were challenging the sovereign State of South Carolina.

The governor of South Carolina, James F Byrnes, said he would spend millions to make colored schools equal—but he would never integrate. This took us to a three-judge court in Charleston where we would have to prove that segregation actually did harm to our clients.

We brought Doctor Kenneth Clark, a social psychologist from New York, down to Clarendon County.

He got off the train with these.

(THURGOOD *goes to the table and removes a white doll and a black doll from his briefcase.*)

Doctor Clark went to the Scotts Branch School with a court order and the two dolls.

(*A photograph of a black child at a school desk fills the wall.* THURGOOD *sits with the dolls before him.*)

Tell me, son, what color is this doll?

What color is this doll?

Which doll looks most like you?

Which doll would you like to play with?

Which doll do you like the most?

Which doll don't you like?

(*The child indicates the brown doll.* THURGOOD *absorbs this, then rises and addresses the court.*)

Your honors, Doctor Kenneth Clark has testified that when the Negro children were asked to choose between the white doll and the brown doll and to say which doll was nice, sixty-five percent said the white doll was the nice doll. Seventy percent of these children thought the brown doll was "bad".

Every one of our tests shows an unmistakable preference for the white doll and a rejection of the brown doll. This overwhelmingly suggests that segregation has a detrimental effect on the personality development of these Negro children. They, like other human beings who are subjected to an inferior status, are irreparably harmed.

And consider the moral confusion of the white children. The white child sees the same people who teach him about democracy, also teach him to discriminate.

Governor Byrnes tells us he will spend millions to make South Carolina's colored schools equal in the future. He says, "All we ask for is time". The Fourteenth Amendment to the Constitution of the United States—ratified in 1868 by all the states including South Carolina—guarantees rights in the present, not at some time in the future.

If the Negro children of Clarendon County are entitled to any rights as American citizens, they are entitled to those rights now. Now is the time for the court to act. Now is the time to end this injustice.

Well, that three-judge court acted, all right. Judge Waring voted for us, but the other two slammed us, ruling for South Carolina—citing Plessy v. Ferguson. They said that having separate schools for black children and white children does not violate the Fourteenth Amendment, and the state should be provided time to make schools equal.

This hit me right in the gut. I really believed we were going to win. The local newspapers were crowing, as if keeping school children segregated was going to save America.

So, while South Carolina took its time, Negro children would suffer day after day in those doghouse schools.

I have to tell you, sometimes I get a little weary of trying to save the white man's soul.

(He rises and paces with restored energy.)

On June 9, 1952 the Supreme Court announced they would hear our appeal of the South Carolina case, along with school cases we had in Kansas, Delaware, Virginia and the District of Columbia. These cases were bundled together and called Brown v. the Board of Education. So, little Harry Briggs Jr is headed to the Supreme Court.

We spent the next six months preparing. We had the best damn team of lawyers you could ask for, a lot of them trained right here at Howard by Charlie Houston.

But many Negroes thought we were wrong going to the Supreme Court and challenging segregation head on. They say if we lose, we're back in the ditch for another twenty years.

We had a big debate right here at Howard where everyone had their say. I knew it was time to roll the dice.

"Brothers and Sisters, this is 1952—three hundred years since we were brought here on slave ships. Nearly a hundred years since the Emancipation Proclamation. Do you want to wait forever? If we don't challenge segregation head-on we will continue to get the same thing we've been getting—separate but un-equal. The N A A C P made a decision to strike down segregation and we will go where we said we would go. I say, damn the torpedoes. Let the Supreme Court decide."

You know who Governor Byrnes enlisted to represent South Carolina? None other than John W Davis, the lawyer's lawyer.

Davis believed the law was on his side. He said, "It's wrong for nine men in Washington to tell a man in South Carolina who his daughter has to sit next to in school".

I climbed those steps to the Supreme Court on a cold, rainy December morning. I saw a line of people stretched all the way down the steps toward the Capitol dome—most of them were black and poor—and counting on us. I stared at those words carved in stone, Equal Justice Under Law. I sure hope so.

VOICE OVER: All rise! The Honorable, the Chief Justice and the Associate Justices of the Supreme Court of the United States Oyez! …Oyez! …Oyez! …All persons having business before the Supreme Court of the United States are invited to draw near and give their attention, for the Court is now sitting. God save the United States and this Honorable Court.

THURGOOD: May it please the Court? I speak on behalf of Harry Briggs, Jr. and the Negro school children of Clarendon County who have raised their attack on the validity of the South Carolina Code that states, "It shall be unlawful for pupils of one race to attend the schools provided for persons of another race".

In the lower courts, we produced unchallenged experts who testified that segregation destroys the self-respect of Negro children and stamps them with a badge of inferiority.

Under our form of government, the only testing ground as to whether or not the majority violates individual rights…is in this, the Supreme Court of the United States.

The Court must weigh the rights of these Negro children against the state policy of South Carolina, and if that policy violates their rights, then this Court is obliged to say, reluctantly or otherwise, that that policy has run up against the Fourteenth Amendment which guarantees to all citizens equal treatment under the law… (Interrupted) Yes, Justice Reed. The state does have responsibility to maintain law and order, and I

believe... *(Interrupted)* No, Justice Frankfurter, it would
not be gerrymandering of school districts. We would...
(Interrupted) Sir, I think what's important is to establish
the principle...segregation by race is not legal.

Sir, it would be impossible, right now, to say precisely
how it would work.

Frankfurter shot back at me. "It is very important,
Mister Marshall, to know before one starts out, where
one is going."

You have less than an hour to make your case. The
justices can interrupt whenever they please and they
really peppered me. They interrupted me forty-three
times. I had this one opportunity to convince them that
segregation was morally wrong, and I got unhinged by
their questions.

(THURGOOD *takes a black leather folder marked "John W
Davis" and opens it.)*

John W Davis had argued a hundred and thirty-eight
cases before the Supreme Court, more than any lawyer
in history except for Daniel Webster. He spoke softly as
if to old friends.

"May it please the court. The resolution proposing the
Fourteenth Amendment was proffered by Congress
in June 1866. One month later, the same Congress
proceeded to establish separate schools for the races
right here in the District of Columbia, and from that
good day to this Congress has not wavered in the
policy. So, clearly, the Congress does not believe that
the Constitution speaks against segregated schools.
In Plessy vs. Ferguson, and in six subsequent decisions
by this Court—nothing can be found that modifies the
doctrine of separate but equal.
So, your Honors, I might ask why should this be a
matter of great national policy? Is it not a fact that the
very strength and fiber of our federal system is local

self-government? Of all the activities of government, is not the one that most nearly approaches the hearts and minds of people...the question of the education of their young?
I respectfully submit that there is no reason this court should reverse the findings of ninety years."

When Davis walked out of that court, he said to Governor Byrnes: "I think we've got it won. Six to three. Maybe five to four. In the language of General Stonewall Jackson— We have got them and they will never see home."

(Projection of the Washington, D C Mall on a rainy night, the Lincoln Memorial in the distance.)

That night I walked the streets in the rain. No hat, no coat, no pride—remembering those days I'd come over from Howard and stand in the back of the chamber.
I thought about the people lined up in the rain that morning and Harry Briggs Junior and the other children in doghouse schools. They were counting on me. The most important goddamn case of the century and what do I do? I get tangled up by their questions.

It made me think of what Charlie Houston used to tell us: "The difference between doctors and lawyers is, doctors can bury their mistakes".

When I got back to the hotel with my chin on the floor, Buster took one look at me and said, "Thurgood, pull up your socks".

More than anything, Buster and I had been wanting a family, and she breaks the news that she's pregnant. Of course, first thing I say is, "We'll name him Thurgood!"

She says, "What if it's a girl?"

"If it's a girl we'll still call him Thurgood."

We went back to New York to wait for the decision.

As Chief Justice Vinson and the other justices weighed our case, outside pressure mounted. Some governors came right out and said they would resist any order to integrate their schools. So people began to ask, "What happens if the court issues an opinion and the states refuse to obey? The Supreme Court doesn't have an army".

You know how we Negroes claim we have a sixth sense for detecting whether a white person is for us or against us? My sixth sense told me that Chief Justice Vinson was not my friend.

All this time, my office at the Legal Defense Fund was fighting discrimination wherever we found it.

I had a big file called "Soldier Trouble". We got complaints from Korea about the treatment of Negro soldiers serving under MacArthur.

You remember General Douglas MacArthur? "Old Soldiers never die, they just fade away." You may not know this, but during World War Two Negro soldiers were assigned to segregated units commanded by white officers. After the war President Truman made a lot of people unhappy by signing an executive order desegregating all the armed forces. General MacArthur just never got around to obeying that order. We had reports that thirty-nine Negro soldiers from the 24th Infantry had been court-martialed for cowardice and disobeying orders and three were sentenced to life in prison in trials lasting less than ten minutes.

So the N A A C P decided I should go out to Korea. I guess they thought I was expendable. When I applied for a passport I found out that MacArthur had called the F B I asking for information about my sex life and what he referred to as my "communist affiliations". I got the passport but the general and I weren't off to a very good start.

I knew men in the 24th Infantry. One man, Lieutenant Leon Gilbert, who had two Bronze Stars, led his thirty-five men up a hill called Bloody Ridge three times and lost thirty of them. A white captain ordered him to go back up the hill with the surviving men. He said, "Sir, if I can't take that hill with thirty-five men, I'll never take it with four". Four nights later, Lieutenant Gilbert was court-martialed and sentenced to death by firing squad.

I finally get to MacArthur's headquarters in Japan. He walks in wearing sunglasses and a chest full of medals.

"Marshall. You should get over to Korea and get a look at some combat."

I know *he* thought I was expendable.

I get to Korea and I'm riding in a jeep with my escort, Colonel D D Martin. Shells start coming in on us, exploding like hell, everybody runs for cover.

Colonel Martin dives into a ditch.

"Where is he? Where's Thurgood?"

"Underneath you, Goddamnit! I don't need no instruction on how to run!"

I finish my investigation and go back to MacArthur. I remind the general that the United States Navy has integrated, and it took the Air Force one day to end discrimination—they gave an order and it happened.

He tells me, "At such time as I find Negroes who are qualified they will be integrated, but not before".

"General, I just talked to a Negro sergeant who'd killed more of the enemy than anyone else in his command. He's not qualified?"

"No."

"General, remember yesterday you had that beautiful brass band playing on your parade ground?"

"Yes," he says, "wasn't that wonderful?"

"Yes, it was delightful. But, there wasn't a single Negro in that band. General, just between you and me, goddamnit, don't you tell me you can't find a Negro who can blow a horn."

Everyone knows war is hell. But in Korea I learned what a special hell it is for brave men to fight and die overseas for freedoms they've never known at home.

We were able to get Lieutenant Gilbert's sentence commuted, but he still had to serve five years in prison.

I was six thousand miles from home when I got word from Buster that we'd lost the baby. We'd tried everything. This was our third miscarriage. On that long plane ride home, I added it up. I'd been on the road more than two hundred nights that year. Away from your wife that much—not the best way to be a good husband.

Then, a bombshell. The Court ordered both sides to come back and re-argue the case, focusing on this question: "What evidence is there that the framers of the Fourteenth Amendment contemplated that it would outlaw segregation in public schools?"

I'd had clients on death row who got saved by a governor with a stay of execution. Now I understood how they felt. We had a second chance. Soon our offices were full of scholars and lawyers researching the history of the states that ratified the Fourteenth Amendment.

And we were running out of money. I spent half my time on the phone begging for help.

One night at home I notice something.

"Buster, where are your pearl earrings?"

"I sold them."

"Sold them?"

"I sent the money to the N A A C P."

"I don't want you selling your jewelry."

"Thurgood, what if your mother hadn't sold her rings? Where would you be today?"

You see, Buster had her own way of sending me to the furnace room.

We were doing late night sessions and a young lawyer had come on board, a white guy from Texas named Black. Charlie Black. Some of our guys worried about having him in our strategy sessions, suspicious of his Texas roots. One night Bob Carter says in front of everybody, "I've been meaning to ask you, Mister Black, why with all the opportunities before you, did you end up working here at the N A A C P for two hundred dollars a month?"

"Well, I'll tell you. I come from deep, deep in Texas— so deep that I can't even remember hearing the word Republican before I was eighteen years old. But I had heard of this really terrible organization up North called the N A A C P. It was an awful place with a great big office way up there in New York City. And the worst thing of all was that right in that big office there was this room, this special secret room with no windows and no doors and walls about a foot thick—and the only way you could get in was with a combination to this huge lock. And inside that room, they said, there was nothing but hooks on the walls— hundreds and hundreds of hooks.

And do you know what was hanging on each and every one of those hooks?

Why…they said that on each of those hooks was a key to the bedroom of a Southern white woman.

And so I figured that's the kind of organization I want to get involved in!"

Then, one more bombshell...a call at midnight... Chief Justice Vinson has died of a heart attack.

So now we start thinking about who President Eisenhower will appoint as the new Chief Justice.

Four days before the opening of the new term, we got our answer. It seems Ike made a deal at the Republican Convention. He promised the next vacancy on the court to California's governor, Earl Warren.

Warren was the man who, during World War Two, sent eighty thousand Japanese American Citizens living in California to internment camps.

Would he be your choice?

I told Buster I was going to make the most of this second chance.

(The marble façade of the Supreme Court fills the back wall.)

VOICE OVER: God save the United States and this Honorable Court.

THURGOOD: John W Davis let everyone know this was his swan song—his last argument before the Court. You could see great esteem for him in the faces of the nine justices.

"May it please the court. Your Honors, the old horn doesn't honk as loud as it used to, but I hope you can hear me.

In Clarendon School District Number One in South Carolina, the state has now provided the Negro children with schools that are equal in every respect. In fact because of their being newer, they may be even better than the schools for the white children. Who would want to disturb this situation?

There are two thousand seven hundred and ninety
registered Negro children of school age in Clarendon
County.

There are two hundred and ninety whites. If you took
the Negro children and co-mingled them with the
white children, you would have, in each classroom,
twenty-seven Negro children and three white children.
Would that make the children any happier? Would
they learn more quickly?

Your Honors cannot sit as a glorified Board of
Education for South Carolina.

We think it a thousand pities that South Carolina might
be ordered to abandon that which it has created.

South Carolina has equal education, not prophesized
but present. I suggest it should not be thrown away on
some fancied question of racial prestige.

It is not my place to offer advice to the learned counsel
on the other side. No doubt they believe what they
propose is best. But I urge them to remember the age-
old motto— 'the best is often the enemy of the good.'"

When he finished, the old man had tears in his eyes. So
did one or two of the justices.

(THURGOOD *opens a leather binder.*)

May it please the Court, as I understand the position of
the distinguished defense counsel, his justification for
segregation in South Carolina is, one, that they just got
together and decided amongst themselves that it is best
for the races to be separated and, two, that segregation
has existed for over a century. Neither argument, to my
mind, is any good.

The Negroes who are forced to submit to segregation
are all American citizens who, by accident of birth, are
a different color. Color makes no difference insofar as
this Court is concerned.

The Fourteenth Amendment was put into our Constitution after a bloody civil war. The duty of enforcing it is placed upon this Court to make sure that the states disregard little pet feelings about race.

Harry Briggs, Jr is guaranteed twelve years of education. There is no way you can repay lost school years...but *they* say, "leave it to the states until they work it out".

The only way this Court can decide this case in opposition to our position is to find that for some reason Negroes are inferior to all other human beings.

Nobody will stand up in this Court and say that, because they would have to justify it.

Only one thing can justify continued segregation—a determination that the people who were once in slavery shall be kept as near that condition as is possible.

Now is the time, we submit, that this Court should make it clear that that is not what the Constitution of the United States stands for.

Now it was in their hands. We had months to wait and waiting makes me itchy.

I worried about Chief Justice Warren. He was a politician who'd never served on a court before—his judicial philosophy was unknown.

I found out later that during the court's deliberations, Chief Justice Warren made a trip to the Civil War battlefields. His chauffeur, a Negro who'd fought in World War Two, drove him to Gettysburg and Warren contemplated the graves and studied the monument with Lincoln's simple words.

On the way home Warren stopped at a Virginia inn for the night. The next morning he comes out and sees his car parked under a tree. He sees the chauffeur asleep in the back seat. He woke him. "Why are you sleeping in the car?"

"Mister Justice, there's no place within twenty miles of here where I can get a room."

Late one night in May, I get a tip on the phone. I was on the first train to Washington and I practically ran from Union Station to the court. Then I was climbing those marble steps...huffing a little.

"Equal Justice Under Law." We'll see.

VOICE OVER: God save the United States and this Honorable Court.

THURGOOD: I stood in the back of the crowded chamber and watched the nine justices file in. Earl Warren opened a black leather folder and I listened to the voice of the Chief Justice of the United States:

(THURGOOD *listens.*)

EARL WARREN VOICE: *(Recorded)* "I have for announcement the opinion of the court in Brown v. the Board of Education. In approaching this question, we cannot turn the clock back to 1868 when the Fourteenth Amendment was adopted, or even to 1896 when Plessy vs. Ferguson was written.

We must consider public education in the light of its present place in American life. Only in this way can it be determined if segregation in public schools deprives these young plaintiffs of the equal protection of the laws.

In these days, it is doubtful that any child may reasonably be expected to succeed in life if he is denied an education. Such an opportunity is a right which must be made available to all on equal terms.

We come to the question: Does segregation of children in public schools solely on the basis of race, even though the physical facilities may be equal, deprive

the children of the minority group of equal educational
opportunities?

We believe…unanimously…that it does.

We conclude that in the field of public education, the
doctrine of `separate but equal' has no place.

Separate educational facilities are inherently unequal.

Therefore, we hold that the plaintiffs are deprived of
the equal protection of the laws guaranteed by the
Fourteenth Amendment.

It is so ordered."

(THURGOOD *absorbs the consequence of the words. He
moves downstage, reflecting on the moment.)*

THURGOOD: Seventeen May, 1954. The highest court
in the nation ruled that America could no longer
humiliate its colored citizens by setting them apart.

Earl Warren led the justices to a unanimous decision—
believing the Court's unity would send a signal to the
nation.

The next day I told the *New York Times* I expected
school segregation in America would be ended in five
years. Over with, finished.

Then, the governor of Virginia announced he would
use "every legal means" to continue segregated
schools. And Strom Thurmond led ninety-seven
Congressmen to sign a Southern Manifesto vowing
to defy the Supreme Court. I felt it was President
Eisenhower's duty to stand up and tell the country
that *Brown* is the law of the land and use his executive
power to enforce the decision. But you know what Ike
said when they asked what he thought? He said he
didn't have an opinion one way or the other.

If Ike had fought World War II the way he fought for
civil rights, we'd all be speaking German today.

It meant that our country would have to go through a long and painful process.

There were sit-ins, marches and bus boycotts. We worked around the clock getting protesters out of jail.

Martin Luther King was a great leader but he'd dump all his legal work on us—including the bills. I used to have a lot of fights with Martin about his theory of disobeying the law. I didn't believe in that. My approach was to use the law, not break it. I told him, "You have two rights. You have a right to disobey the law; you also have the right to go to jail for it".

Martin kept talking to me about Henry David Thoreau's theory of *Civil Disobedience*—and I'd remind him that Thoreau wrote *Civil Disobedience* in jail.

(THURGOOD *turns upstage and moves to a chair where he sits silently for a moment.*)

I knew Buster hadn't been well during the school cases, but she'd always insist she was well enough to go down to Washington to be in court with me. Except for the decision…she didn't make that trip. It was then, when she could no longer hide it, that I found out how sick she really was. She said she hadn't wanted to add to my burden.

What kind of man has a wife dying of cancer and doesn't know it.

She was gone in six months. Buster died on February 11th…her forty-fourth birthday.

I didn't know what to do. I'd never been alone before. Uncle Fearless was gone. My Daddy was gone. Charlie Houston was gone.

With Buster gone I lost thirty pounds. Kept a bottle in my desk for company. I was rude and irritable; nobody wanted to be around me. Eventually I poured myself back into my work.

Resistance to the Supreme Court decision meant we had to pull up our socks and go into courtrooms all over the south.

The school decision gave us a precedent—we had a foot in the door. Now, equal means *integrated*. We could challenge segregation of libraries, restaurants and public toilets. When I was a boy in Baltimore there were very few public toilets for colored people. So when you felt something, the only thing you could do was to jump on the trolley for home and hope.

I remember one day...I got off the trolley and only made it as far as the front door of our house. That's more than an inconvenience. You never forget something like that.

It came too late for my mother and my daddy, but those old "White Only" signs in Baltimore were finally coming down.

It had been five years since the Brown case and I decided it was time to stop traveling a hundred thousand miles a year and to go into some big law firm and do something I'd never managed to do—make myself a bunch of money.

I'd started seeing Cecilia Suyat who worked in our office. Cissy had a sense of humor that kept me in line. In time we married and before too long she made me a very happy man—along came Thurgood Junior—he was a boy—and John.

Now, I get a call from the new Attorney General, Robert Kennedy. He tells me President Kennedy has decided to make me a judge on the Federal Court of Appeals—the second highest court in the country.

People call me a liar when I say this, but when I was a young lawyer in Baltimore—my highest aim was to be a county magistrate—like that little teetotaler in Tennessee. Back then there were only two Negro judges in the entire country.

The Chief Judge of the Court made my swearing-in in New York a nice deal and arranged a group photo of all the judges. Just before everyone arrived the photographer took a test shot and blew a fuse.

(The stage goes dark.)

A few minutes later I walk in. People are milling around in the dark and this flustered secretary sees me.

"Oh, thank God. The electrician!"

"Lady, you must be crazy if you think a colored man could become an electrician in New York City."

At first, I was low man on the court dealing with the least interesting cases, like taxes and corporate law. And I got all the Wall Street securities cases because the other judges owned stocks and had conflicts of interest. I used to say, "How nice it must be for you boys to have a poor man on the bench to handle this stuff."

But, let the record show, I wrote ninety-eight majority opinions and not a one of them was reversed by the Supreme Court.

One day I'm in the judges' dining room and a bailiff runs in, "Judge, Judge!"

"Fred, I told you not to bother me when I'm eating."

"The President wants to talk to you."

"The president of what?"

"The President of the *United States*. Lyndon Johnson."

"Judge Marshall, I want you to be the Solicitor General of the United States."

"Oh, why, thank you sir. That's a great honor. I'd like some time to talk to Mrs. Marshall."

"You take just as much time as you need."

Next morning I get to the office, the phone rings. It's L B J.

"Mister President, you said I'd have all the time I needed."

"You've *had* time!"

"Number one, sir, it's a salary loss of five thousand dollars."

"I know that."

"Number two, I'd be giving up a lifetime job on the court."

"I know that."

"And finally, I haven't got any money."

"I know that too. I've got your tax return right in front of me."

Then, right over the phone, Lyndon B Johnson took me by the ears.

"Thurgood, I want people to go in the Supreme Court and see a black man standing there in the Solicitor's cutaway coat and say, 'Who is that Negro up there?' and hear the answer: 'He is the Solicitor General of the United States.'"

By the time L B J got finished with me I was ashamed I hadn't volunteered.

So, Cissy and the boys, we moved down to Washington. This Pullman-car waiter's son was about to become the highest-ranking Negro ever to serve in the United States government.

Now, there had been rumors that if a vacancy came up on the Supreme Court L B J might appoint me. But the politicians were telling Johnson that if he put a Negro on the court it would cost him the South in the '68 election.

The night Justice Tom Clark resigned we went to a party in his honor.

The president pulls me aside and says, "Don't expect the job".

That really put me on my heels. I wanted that job. I thought I'd earned it. But I figured some no good sons of bitches had stoked L B J up with rumors about me and booze and women.

Next day he calls me over to the Oval Office...I figure he'll explain why he isn't appointing me.

"You know something, Thurgood... I'm going to put you on the Supreme Court."

"Why, thank you, Mister President."

"Have you told Cissy?"

"How could I tell Cissy? I didn't know anything. She'll be shocked."

"Well, Goddammit let's get her on the phone and we'll break the news!"

Before you know it the White House operator has Cissy on the speakerphone.

I say, "Hi honey".

Cissy says, "Hi Thurgood. Did we get the Supreme Court appointment?"

You never heard a man laugh the way L B J did.

Then he says, "Thurgood, I guess our friendship is about busted up now. I guess I won't be seeing you much."

"Why, Mister President, Justice Tom Clark stayed best friends with Truman even when he voted against the President's wishes. Clark really socked it to Truman in the steel case. I would have no hesitation socking it to you."

Johnson just stared at me... "You mean you'd do that to me?"

"You bet!"

Then he looked me in the eye and shook my hand. "I'm glad we understand each other."

But those were tough political times. L B J was twisting senators' arms to get me confirmed and it got nasty. The vote was sixty-nine for me, eleven against. Johnson persuaded twenty Southern Democrats not to vote at all—so they could cover their asses for the next election.

Then L B J calls me:

"Congratulations, *Mister Justice Marshall.* But, goddamnit, the hell you caused me! I've never been through such hell."

I was sworn in in the Rose Garden of the White House by my friend, Supreme Court Justice Hugo Black, a former member of the Ku Klux Klan.

(THURGOOD *goes to stage right and an aide helps him put on the black robe of a Supreme Court Justice.)*

I would wear this robe for nearly twenty-five years. The life of a Justice is far different from the hurly burly of the courtroom. To tell you God's truth—I missed the action at first. You hear cases, you read briefs, you think, you meet in conference with the other eight Justices—the most secret and private of all gatherings—and then you think some more and you write. I wrote opinions on three hundred and twenty-two cases.

(He *moves a chair downstage and sits facing the audience.)*

Sitting on that bench listening to cases being argued, my mind often went back to the howls of those prisoners in the Northwest Baltimore Police Station. Which is why I did everything in my power to protect the civil rights of every American citizen.

I say the death penalty is cruel and unusual punishment which is prohibited by the Eighth Amendment. *They* say it's a deterrent. Hell, if it was really a deterrent, there never would have been a second execution after the first one.

As a defense lawyer I fought to get innocent men life imprisonment instead of the gas chamber, which left time for new evidence and appeals. I was the only one on the court who'd ever tried a murder case, and I'd seen too many innocent defendants sentenced to death.

Think about this—there are seventy countries in the world that forbid capital punishment. Wouldn't America pay herself the highest tribute by recognizing the humanity of our fellow human beings by settling for life imprisonment without parole?

On the Warren Court we put a stop to all executions in 1967, but then Nixon was elected and he was able to appoint four justices in just four years. So the executions began all over again. I was writing a dissent in every death penalty case that came before us. By that time most of the other justices were so close, they were peeing through the same quill.

I left instructions for my clerks to wake me at any hour if a request came in for a stay of execution. I also told them, "If I die, prop me up and keep on voting!"

And I am for gun control. Complete gun control. I don't see why any private citizen needs to carry a pistol or a machine gun.

During the school cases we had some mean phone calls in New York. One night the Chief of Police invites me for a drink. He says, "Thurgood, we're worried about you". And he hands me this little package wrapped as a gift.

I open it up and there's a .32 and some ammunition. I hand it right back to him. "Chief—my weapon is the law. I'll just have to do the best I can with that."

I wrote opinions based on the First Amendment. I believe that whatever justifications there may be for states regulating obscenity, they do not reach into the privacy of one's own home. If the First Amendment means anything, it means that a state has no business telling a man, sitting alone in his own house, what books he can read or what films he can watch. Our constitutional heritage rebels at the thought of giving government the power to control men's minds.

We had to screen some pornographic movies in one of these cases. That was a fun assignment. At the end I turned to the Chief Justice.

"Did you learn anything new from that one? I didn't."

When you're named to the Supreme Court it's a lifetime job, but presidents just love making Supreme Court appointments. And they can't do that unless there's an empty seat.

In the spring of 1970 I got a bad case of pneumonia and went into Bethesda Naval Hospital. The word got around that I was sicker than most people realized. I get feeling a little better and the head of the hospital comes in.

"Mister Justice, we have a request for a report on your condition—and I wouldn't think of releasing it without your permission."

"Who wants it?"

"President Nixon."

"Okay, you go ahead. You can release it, providing you write in big letters at the bottom, Not Yet, Goddamit!"

During the Reagan years a lot of people wanted me off the court. Too old, too liberal, too tipsy. I'd tell them I accepted a lifetime appointment and I'm going to stay for life. I expect to die at the age of a hundred and ten—shot by a jealous husband.

You should know Cissy used to get after me about being too soft on our boys. And I'd get defensive. "I'm not going to punish those boys for something that I ever did."

"Then you'll never punish them for anything because you've done everything."

(He rises and walks slowly to the podium at the center of the table.)

Well, one day—it was my last day on the court, but no one knew that—I took off my robe and walked around the bench and I'm standing right where I stood when I argued the school case.

I address my fellow justices: "May it please the court, I stand here with my son, Thurgood Marshall, Jr, and my daughter in law, Colleen Mahoney. Honorable Justices, I am here to vouch for their standing as lawyers and to recommend their admission to the bar of the Supreme Court of the United States."

Sitting in the third row with Cissy was my other son, John—a United States Marshall, a man of the law.

Would it be bragging if I told you that was the proudest day of my life?

(THURGOOD picks up his cane from the table and moves downstage.)

So, Cissy and I made a decision. I've given fifty years to the law and this is it.

(He looks, waiting for questions—his last press conference.)

What?

The most important?

Well, two cases—beating the Texas white primary voting system, Smith v. Allwright, and Brown v. Board of Education.

But the sweetest was getting Donald Gaines Murray into the University of Maryland Law School. I was young and hungry for revenge.

What?

Should a Negro replace me?

The President appoints justices, I don't. I'd be opposed to picking the wrong Negro and saying, "I'm picking him because he's a Negro". My daddy told me there's no difference between a white snake and a black snake. They both bite.

I've always believed the whole thrust of our Constitution is people to people. Strike them and they will cry; cut them and they will bleed; starve them and they will whither away and die.

But treat them with respect and decency, give them equal access to the levers of power, attend to their aspirations and grievances, and they will flourish and grow...and, yes, join together to form a more perfect union.

Sure, we know how far we've come—but we also know how far we still have to go. I may have "retired" written after my name, but I'm going to stay in this fight—until the following thing happens.

That is that on some day in the future, on the commuter train to New York coming through

Connecticut picking up wealthy people, bringing them
down to Wall Street, and on this day to come, a Negro
gets on the train up around Fairfield with his Brooks
Brothers suit, derby hat, dispatch case banged up
just enough, Wall Street Journal under one arm, and
the train moves, stop-by-stop picking up people, and
eventually it gets crowded. And a white woman gets
on near the last stop, and she goes up and down the
car, and there's only one empty seat, and that's beside
this Negro. The woman sits down in this one empty
seat.

And then, she just can't take it any more, and she yells
out, "Niggers! Niggers! Niggers!"

(He leaps to his feet.)

And then the Negro jumps up and says, "Where!
Where! Where!"

Our country?

My schoolmate, Langston Hughes, said it pretty well.

Oh, let America be America again.
The Land that never has been yet—
And yet must be—the land where
—every man is free.
The land that's mine—the poor man's,
—Indian's, Negro's, ME—
Whose sweat and blood, whose faith and pain
Must bring back our mighty dream again.
Oh yes.
I say it plain.
America never was America to me.
And yet, I swear this oath—
America will be.

(THURGOOD *exits.*)

END OF PLAY